THE UNFATHOMABLE
Holocaust and After

Vivian Kearney

PUKIYARI PUBLISHERS
www.pukiyari.com

To the memory of victims of hate and all
who suffer from their loss.
To Freda, my mother, and the families who rescued me.
To Milo, my husband, our children Sean and Kathleen
and their spouses Lisa and Danny,
and our grandchildren, Ben, Eli, Jeremy, Ian and Collin
- with love and gratefulness

Table of Contents

Destroyed

Past to Present

Let my tears
Become stars
To guide you

Posing for a Portrait in Warsaw Around 1936

Right after we take the portrait
Let's go by the market -
Rosa's coming this Friday night
We'll have a little *Shabbes*
Mame and *Tate* would be happy to know that
Though they never want to visit
Our modern Warsaw
That offers so many opportunities
With this new enlightened society
We're ready for the world
And the dear, lovely world
Is ready for us

What bright trust
Broken in a few moments
A few years' time
That transformed them into ashes
Vaporizing in metallic skies
That fertilized the waiting landscape
But got into
The eyes of our souls
Forever tearing in submerged grief
And attempted remembering

Technicolor It Happened

Technicolor it happened
Not the black and white
Of old movies
Not the dark letters
Of shaming documents
Not the blurred shadows
Of unspeakable documentaries
Not the brown, beige and grey
Of our pictured memorials

The grass was green, the sky blue
The stars yellow
The buildings friendly, the streets familiar
The chasers were people too

The victims were our families, friends
Neighbors

The roads still seemed possible
But the trains, guns and gas chambers
Were suddenly there also
To take away
Life's colors

Gone

Unknowing and unknown
The hopes in their eyes
The smiles, the seriousness
Of forging a good religious
Or secular life

Now gone those ideals and goals
Of a generation
That struggled to be
Consilient with modern times
And their parents'
Village-roofed
Universe

Dispersed in the smoke
Ashes and mud
Slide into

The unfathomable

Memorial

They

Went away in trains
Trailing smoke clouds
Of an angry world

The surprised victims
Who had been living
Millions of variegated lives

Now we

Read mournfully
Some of their stories and hear echoes
Of their receding voices and wonder

Is there a Warsaw, a Vilna, a *shtetl* in heaven
So they can continue conversing
In that philosophical, emotive
Stabbed Yiddish language?

For us to look up and hear
After weaving our word wreaths
To honor, to revive, to remember

Them

What Next?

The world I carry with me
My backpack of memories, thoughts
Containing treasures of relations
Albums of conversations
Colors seen, melodies heard, books read
Plus the tapes in my head
Maps of roads given, chosen, envisioned...

What will become of this cherished world?
What will be left
After the holocaust
Of death?

A Riddle

Civilizations with many societies
Societies with multiple populations
Populations composed of myriad individuals
Each individual storing diverse facts,
Histories, emotions, interests
Each interest a galaxy of connections

So, how many societies, persons, facts,
Emotions, interests, connections
Have been destroyed or wounded
And haunt our civilization?

Death Don't Celebrate

Death, don't celebrate
Though you are a force, a whirlpool
A malevolent vapor
A destroyer of present life
Yet the grass comes back

Electric connections
Collectivized as soul, mind, will, character
Of people past and present
Can walk the earth
And the heavens

As does God, the undeniable
Undieable
Existence-Creator

Smokestacks

Clay leaves and stone sky
Mud for our abandoned shoes
No more walking into the future or living in the past
Oxygen for our dreams has been gassed away
No more learning, no roles to fulfill, no careers to try
No more place on earth for us

Never Again

When you contemplate
The results of hate
However mandated
By self-regard

Let yourself be moved
Let your mind be nauseated
Let your heart say
May it never again
Be done by me or by anyone else

Adonai, Rabbeinu shel olam
Lord of the universe
With Thy help

Picture It

Shoes

Picture of shoes, all those useful shoes
Mountains of abandoned shoes
Doesn't heartsicken quite so much
To contemplate
If you can't imagine
Who stopped wearing them
And why

Children Being Led Through the Woods

Kinderlech, children
Where are you going?

In your flimsy clothes
With guards at your sides
In great overcoats

We don't know
We're too scared to ask
Or to cry

The forest is dim
This walk isn't fun
When the path stops
We think our lives are done

We thought we'd grow
To understand this world
Now we think
We're going to a place
Of no tomorrows

Kinderlech, children
Your lives may be short
But don't forget
You've been good children
It's not your fault

The woods are lovely
But Mama, I don't want to sleep

Maybe the kinder trees and softer ground
Will sing *kaddish* for us

Striped - after the movie *The Boy in the Striped Pyjamas*

Two eight-year old boys
Sitting the same way
Both with floppy ears
One with dark hair
One with none
One with politely chewing teeth
One with none
One in neat clothes
With a good sweater
The other in black and white
Striped garb

Two sides of Germany
Separated and destroyed
By barbed wire and gas ovens
Ashes and bitterness
For both sides
For how long?

What do we do
With our black-white natures?
Is anyone good enough
To overcome our
Sometimes murderous selfishness
With compassion?

Who can save us

From our shadow selves
And inject us
With more kindness DNA
And take away
Those judging, sentencing
Stripes

Snatched Away

So many unresolved issues
How can we leave?
So many words unsaid
How can we die?
So many souls taken by the Reaper
Where in the clouds of hereafter?
So many secrets to find out

So many ways to mourn -
Don't criticize mine

Lechayim - To Life - after the movie *Life is Beautiful*

After the holocaust
What can we do
To continue saying
Lechayim - to life?

And then,
How can you get rid of evil?
Should you dance on tragic cliffs
Proclaiming that, nevertheless,
Life is wonderful and blessed?

Can sheltering secrets really
Fight the wrongs, heal the wounds
Allowing our souls to reach above
To an overarching, forgiving love?

Echoes - after the movie *Sarah's Key*

What can express survivor guilt
Of violence's later victims
Those new prisoners
Of past prejudice

Living in echo chambers of self-hatred
Afraid to open closets
Although the keys remain
Locked in our scabbed hearts

Just leave, just go
To another continent
Dance, work and write every given moment

Remodel the shadow box
Minimize the elephants in the room
Sweep rhinoceri under the carpet
Create a new life

What can explain
The present blessings
Contrasting with
God's absence in the war

Why didn't He send
More angels at the right time
To rescue all targeted for expulsion
From ambitious countries

Reasons plod wearily
Philosophies become cynical
Strands of biographies shine
But remain unwoven
Identities start and restart
Secrets fester while onlookers
Prefer not to open decomposing rooms

Yet - a wounded hand, an opened door, mentoring letters
A sympathetic embrace, a bouquet, an angelic nurse
Shards of daylight in the dark

Give clues about the ultimate reality -
Courageous charity

Haunted

More Questions, One Answer

When does the haunting end?
Will we ever be healed?
Or forever the wounds continue?

Questions sent into the ether
From each walking this pilgrim world
Who can hear, who can receive the answer?

Don't wait, be still and serve

Contrasts

Amazing the blessings
The graces, the mercies
The miracles, the wonders,
The beauties, the interests
The adventures, connections
For us

But why not for them?
Why were they packed into trains?
Pushed into hatred's implacable camps?

As offerings
Victims of power's cancers
Their souls still reverberating, questioning
With ours

Survivor Guilt in the Gym

How they would have loved this
Warm water poured on frozen fingers
Machines to tune up myriad muscles
Lights and music
One opportunity
After another

Why was I given all this?
Instead of their misery

Too tragic
To contemplate for longer than it takes
To wash my hands

Why their lack of
Such loving chances?

Plus

I'm so sorry
I'm not the six million
Plus uncountable others...
Yet

People All

A Velt Mit Veltlech - A World With Many Little Worlds

Every person is a landmark
An old oak tree for others
To hang their paradigm looms
Their harps of stories
Identity mirrors

A guard light for many lights - a *shomer*
A world made up
Of many little worlds
A velt mit veltlech

Grandparents

Working hands
Folded and still
Then for an hour
Now motionless as a picture
On a yellow wall
In a house about to be sold
Retooled and retold
In Montreal
A city of subways, cars and buses

So far
Far away from
The horse-plodding village
Of Big Eyes - *Wielke Oczy*
Two lakes once looking up to heaven
In Poland

The grandparents posing
From their about to be
Anthologized, archeologized
Abandoned village
With its bearded and head-scarved
Devout and devoted
Tradition

Believe

Ann Frank
So frank
About your caged
Teenage years

Do you still trust
That people really are good
Deep inside
Or want to be?

After what happened to you
Was it all a nightmare?
Do you still believe
From above?

Let me believe for you
Here below

Missing the Unknown Family

We could have read their journals, letters
We could have heard their sagas
And therein found our places

We could have exchanged gifts
We could have listened to their advice
And seen similarities of characters and faces

We could have compared notes and lessons
We could have shared *naches* - family joys and pride
With the previous generation

We could have chafed at their dictation
But our lost and present families could have
Sailed together
On many voyages of celebration

Survivors

Resignation

The play is finished.
The actors have been called elsewhere.
The audience has mostly dispersed.
We have left the interactive dramas
With our previous generation

The candles of their past hopes
For a continued culture have vanished
Into a new age's
Neon laughter

The far away symphonies
Of that tragic time
Still sound faintly

But we have stopped discussing
Their lovely ideals
For a better world
And cried less

After the Heroic Generation

We were defined by a generation
Of voluble, vehement, vociferous
War survivors, ringing the mountain city
With their vivacity, often contentious

Now that these guards are gone
How can we identifiably live?
Yet obliging signs do announce
We have to remember to forgive

Left With

It was the cleaning -
The cleaning and the sewing -
The sewing, the cooking, the eating
That were left to emphasize
To criticize

Once religious observances -
Observances and traditions -
Traditions, cultures and bonds
Were gone or discarded
Left behind

Due to war -
War, destruction and the new era
Modern and generational
Allegiances, goals

And we -
We are the ones
Supposed to celebrate -
Celebrate to make our existence
Right and perfect

Though we are left
With internalized guilts
Guilts of days and years
Confused webs of hopes and guidance
And judgements

Survivor's Challenge From the Other Side

We were smart;
We knew how to talk Polish, French, Yiddish, Ukrainian,
    Russian, a little English

We were clever;
We moved, we sewed, we had good trades

We worked alongside
Our countrymen in the village, in Pzemisch, in Warsaw,
    in Paris, in Montreal

We were kind;
We helped family, friends, neighbors, acquaintances,
    strangers

We read a lot and knew all the news;
We celebrated Chanukah, Pesach, the end of the war

We loved life, humanity, knowledge;
We were sensitive to people, nature, art, ideals

We cried
We bled

For we were simply persons
Not power hungry
Not mice to be exterminated

We were adept
At finding the few of us left

And we met all sorts of outstanding Samaritans
Mentshn, upright people, true earth angels

And what is my legacy?
I want you
To remember our stories
And be like us, like those kind ones too.

Kindnesses Encountered

Do you really know
What it feels like
After prison camp life
The blessing
Of a house
That offers you
A bowl of warm soup, hot bread

A prepared table – *shulchan aruch*
That can make you feel like
An approved
Well-regarded
Cherishable
Human

Can you imagine
After the running
The welcoming friends
The overwhelming
Of a bouquet
For my saint's day...
Not even my tradition!

Some Miracles

Door isn't sealed, why don't you jump?
I jumped from the train

Hide in the bushes, though children are playing there
I hid; they threw a ball over me; they didn't see

Maybe, I thought, my parents
Were watching over me

People in the camp were dying every day
But just before I did
I was packed into a farm-bound army truck

As for me, in another prisoner camp,
I got transferred to woodworking

Our home in Paris was occupied by the enemy;
We were hiding in a factory
Impossible to continue, but a saintly family
Invited us to the country

There were miracles
From whom and why?
Whence the angels?

How did we survive?
A grand plan? a strong will to live? chance?
We don't know

Ours to continue working, helping, living
Tomorrow and the following tomorrows

This Baby

My story starts
With a doorstep beginning
Brought out of the ghetto
Placed in an orphanage
Founded by a noteworthy priest
Relocated to various places

Who were there as the first responders
Before I was reunited with family survivors?
Who cared
That this baby should later share
With own children, grandchildren,
Family, others

Poems, stories
From both sides
Of the pit of slaughter

All those mysterious helpers
To find, to meet and to thank

A celebration
Possible only
In the hereafter

Found - Momentos of a Mentor

We had discussed its existence
We had searched for it

Next day I found the paper right there -
Where it wasn't seen before
For some reason
In the middle of the floor

Emotional, poetical
Sorrowful, joyful
Time-yellowed
Yiddish newspaper article
About the writer always being
Heartsick, homesick
For a brother's words

In those treasures of letters
That he recovered, endlessly reread
On home leave from fighting
All so wisely mentoring

And now I can see
Two brothers' characters
Once more revived
With this decades-old clipping's
Surprising reappearance
Witnessing their grace-thirsty questions
And dear reassurance

And Then There Was One - End of an Era

Looming Loss

Raining tears falling
Tearing rains tearing
Us from understandable wharves
That had held us
So comfortingly before

Assisted Living

Your present fragility, mother
Burns a field-wide space
In our souls beyond which
We have never yet travelled

As we fence in
Your plants, steps, schedules, words
So carefully
So you can keep being
Our past, present and future
Matriarch -
The last of our family's
Before the war survivors

Longevity

We tried
To keep you alive
Dear enduring one

Wrapping you tenderly
In considerate secrets

Not realizing
That your history
Also had many blankets

A New Garden

Looking at the brilliant sunrise
As the plane departs
Humming ever more expectantly

Multicolored tears I weep for you
Rainbowed sighs I cry for you

As you wrestle with this old tent
And breathlessly move
Towards a new garden

Do you know, do you trust
That God loves you

Passing

I ran away
From foxes and wolves
From enemies outside
From quandaries inside
From restricting traditions
From trains leading nowhere

Said the panting, stubborn soul
Of a holocaust survivor
And I can and I will
Run away from you
O death

Straight into the arms
Of an invisible God
From whom I first escaped
Before this race began

You Can Read

You can
Read the holocaust
In her eyes

You can
Hear her running
In her labored breathing

You can
Feel her care
In her tired hands

You can
Witness her trying
To keep her earth identity

Even while
Immigrating to
The land of eternity

Inspiring us
To follow her *mitzvot,*
With our own
Good deeds of love
Also

Please Tell Me

Was I a hero?
Trembled the question
From the hospital bed

Especially, uniquely
You were a marvelous *mentsh*
A food and care provider
In the war

Later
A concerned mother
And a working housewife
And a good wife
A torchbearer
Of Yiddish culture
A saga keeper
A solicitous matriarch
A health-conveying cook
Almost to the end
And a great seamstress

Yes, a hero
Granted your family
Plus those around
To help and to bless

Vigil

A vigil hospital side
For a woman we thought
A fortress of survival
Now becoming a tent
Quickly shredding

Tired green eyes
Ears that would not hear
Thirsty mouth that could not drink
Or talk

Letting us hold a priceless
Antique of a still living hand

A long look
Asking for forgiveness
For leaving

Didn't We Witness

When we
Witnessed you struggling
As we sat around your hospital bed
Helplessly

Didn't we see
Your will still fighting

Didn't we argue with you
As you tried to get out
And pleaded to go to work again

Didn't we hear
Your gravelly voice
Bravely joining
Our farewell songs

Didn't we watch
Your mind figuring
How to cope
With an imprisoning bed
With this new stage
This unwanted trip

How could such a definite personality
Evaporate and disappear?

Ani ma'amin - I believe

Your soul
And ours
Always survive

Thank you for your presence
Those last days
Thank you for your life's testimony
That defined us
For so long

So long, dear Freda
Until we meet again

We Had Thought

We had thought they were
Everlasting mountains
Bright fields
Of survivors' picnics

But they turned into cars
Zooming into
The too soon horizon
With bags and baggage
Of experiences
Perceptions, echoing opinions

And we
Were left and became
Orphaned trees instead

Sunflowers

Massive gray cement blocks
On the side of the road
Pavement torn up
Once part of a solid flowing street
Now piled into jagged rock pieces

Several sunflowers
Peek out of the dusty mounds
Their bright yellow-brown faces
Announcing
We're still here

Worn down their bodies
That once housed brave spirits
That once drove down many roads

Now their souls sometimes
Meet me around corners
Waving from highways and byways
Announcing
We still live

Dealing With History

History Approaching

Closer and closer
Comes the history, sometimes
Clamorously
While I
Run and hide

Books Left

Once upon a time
I ambled into a small European bookstore
Saw many old volumes
In Yiddish and Hebrew
Some with happy
Group pictures
Could be our relatives
Left behind

Sold and selling
As now rare
Therefore treasured
Curiosities for
Interesting collections
Of savy collectors

Books Reign

In a southwestern retirement city
Trying to sleep in a comfortable chair
In a school library back corner
Where by coincidence
Holocaust and Second World War books
Reign on the shelves

Retelling the history
Of a life-swallowing tsunami
Some seventy years back
That some and I survived

I snuggle close
Asking for rest
While they remember
And analyze

But I can't -
Not yet
So I walk away

All We Want

Home Internet
Do you remember?
Please describe
Reconstitute the village - the *shtetl*
The names, the fields
The houses, the buildings,
The families, the lives
Don't let them die

In the dust of forgetfulness
Continuously covering the past

For all we each want
Is to live forever

Auld Lang Syne

If I
Tape your names
On a sticker
On a ringbinder
For typed transcriptions
Of your interviews
Decades ago

Then you'll still live
In memory
On paper
In computer ether
And hopefully
Won't be buried
Out of mind
Out of this era
Nor ever
Be forgotten

One Survivor to Another

Wait a minute
I said
To the ghost in the machine

I have to make myself a snack
Get some paper
Sharpen a pencil
Open some windows

Before I continue transcribing, translating
Your memories

That's okay
She said
I died -
I have all the time in the world

However -
You don't

Videotapes of Freda, Stefan, Mania

The high humming sound of
The rewinding old tech videotape
Is like the sound of
The swift, ultra-modern
Subway in Montreal

If you can disregard
Its impersonal, nauseating speed

You can
Close your eyes
See and hear
The survivors' life stations
Rattling by
In a time-space machine
Going forward

First stop - Wielke Oczie and Lastchuf villages *Shtetl*
structures, families, neighbors, Hebrew, Polish
and home education, religious observances,
traditions

Second stop - Warsaw of the big city street - strolls,
discussions, meetings, lectures, sewing and
printing machines modernizing trades,
opportunities and ideals galore

Third stop - the war - ghetto, persecution, violence,
            hunger, sickness, death, scarcity, bombing,
            prisoner camps, escapes, monstrous tragedies,
            hiding, finding a few family and familiar
            souls, realizing the loss

Fourth stop - Paris - free and freeing France, lights, parks,
            beautiful safety, for them Europe at its best

Fifth stop - Montreal years - often fine, sometimes
            wonderful, mostly comfortable, although
            always in mourning for the victims...

Last stop – silence.

Written Words - A Thematic Blessing

Checking each letter, checking the checkers
The old-world *bal-maliach* grandfather,
Examining the new torahs

Learning the words that were so important
That every little *cheder* - nursery school boy
Tasted their letters with apples and honey

Reading and rereading his brother's letters
The now city-boy apprenticed for the printing
Of new ideas

Presently the graphics, the editing, the transcribing
The teaching of reading and essay writings
The histories, articles, analyses, memos, journals
The insomniac meditations turning into poems

A thematic blessing through the generations
Of recollecting, rebuilding words

Past to Future

Night stars, constellations
Tears for the victims
Lights for the generations
Memorials and inspirations

Please stop wars' shame
Please sing *lechayim* - to life -
And Amen

Please spell out God's holy name